FIRST SEASONS

A New Journey

BY MARJORY McKINLEY SPRAYCAR
INTRODUCTION BY JUNE RAY SMITH

FIRST SEASONS PRESS

BALTIMORE, MARYLAND

FIRST SEASONS
A NEW JOURNEY

BY MARJORY MCKINLEY SPRAYCAR

Published by:
FIRST SEASONS PRESS
605 Worcester Road
Baltimore, Maryland 21286-7834

Printed in the United States of America

Design by Isely and/or Clark Design

ISBN 0-9701086-0-5

CONTENTS

INTRODUCTION V

WINTER 1

SPRING 19

SUMMER 37

FALL 53

Introduction

YOU ARE HERE

You've seen these words many times.
But this time the "X" marks a spot you've
never been before. Life as you know it
has completely changed; you're at the
start of your new journey. There are no
maps or directories, no signs to guide
you. You feel alone in uncharted territory.

The crossroads are marked "denial,"
"anger," "bargaining," "depression," and
"acceptance." They will become very
familiar to you during your journey.

All around you people laugh and talk,
cars move along the roadways, couples
walk together, the mail comes. Everyone
seems to know exactly where they're

going and what they should be doing, except you. You feel alone, out of place. You wonder: What will life be like from now on? Will it ever feel normal again? Will I ever be happy again?

Your journey into this new territory will be unique. Don't try to compare it to anyone else's situation or circumstance. You may be sharing it with family and friends, but it is yours alone.

Think of it as a process that will gradually move you away from the pain you feel at the beginning of your journey to a life with new possibilities.

First Seasons is meant to help you along the way with encouragement for finding comfort in all seasons. You'll find ideas for giving comfort to yourself and others. At first you may not be able to think about giving comfort to other people, but eventually you may find that reaching out to others helps give shape and substance to the new life you are building.

On your new journey, keep this book with you. Take comfort from it often.

—JUNE RAY SMITH

Winter

WARMTH FOR THE HEALING HEART

When your new journey actually begins,
it will feel like the worst cold and
barren days of winter no matter what
the actual outside temperature.
So our journey for the healing heart
begins in winter with comforts meant
to give warmth on cold days.
Some of them you'll use when the
cold is coming from the
weather outside; others are meant for
times you're feeling cold inside.

Find a notebook and use it to write down a few things about each day—what you did, who you saw, how you felt. It may help you feel less scattered, help give focus to your daily tasks. From time to time go back and read it. On a bad day it will help you to see that you've had better days. On a good day it will make you appreciate how far you've come.

The shortest day—and longest night—of the year is December 21. Take comfort in knowing after that the days will gradually get longer and brighter. When you're feeling discouraged, remember that progress on you journey will be gradual too.

When you aren't feeling your best but have to keep going, wear comfortable, soft, warm clothes—as close to pajamas as you can get.

Going to bed alone can be lonely if you've usually had someone by your side. To help fill in the emptiness, turn a radio on to play soft music while you fall asleep. Set it to turn off automatically in a half an hour or so.

Put the photo of someone you love in a small frame at your bedside where you can see it first thing in the morning and the last thing at night.

Tell a special friend or relative how much his or her love and support means to you.

Strike a balance in the number of people you come in contact with every day. If you're mostly alone, call someone, take a walk, or go to a library, museum, or mall just to be around other people. If your day includes contact with lots of people, make sure you build some time in your day when you can be alone with yourself.

Does it feel like a part of your life is missing? Don't try to convince yourself otherwise or that you should be able to get on with your life. You are on a very difficult journey. Be patient with yourself.

If your journey started with the death of a life-long partner, the place where your love died—a hospital or hospice—now holds special poignancy for you. Go back there if you can. Take a small thank-you gift to the health professionals you came to know there. You'll find sympathetic listeners who understand what you're going through because they saw it first hand.

Use an answering machine so you won't miss calls from friends who call while you're out. Their voices will make you feel wanted even if you haven't actually connected.

Call a neighbor or friend who you haven't seen for a while just to touch base. You'll both have a sense of security knowing that you are still connected.

When out for your regular walk, say good morning or good evening to other walkers your meet—even if they seem to be ignoring you. It's a small way of feeling connected to other people.

Take a warm bath or shower before bedtime.

For a late afternoon pick-me-up, make a cup of hot cocoa.

Crawl into a warm bed. While you're brushing your teeth and washing your face, put a heating pad or a hot water bottle on the spot where your feet will be.

Resurrect or replace a favorite article of clothing—sweater, jacket, or sweatshirt—something that you once enjoyed wearing. Or wear a favorite sweater or shirt that belonged to someone you love. It will bring you warmth and closeness.

Take a walk and see how many different kinds of evergreen varieties you can find.

When you feel the first signs of a sore throat, turn to soft foods for comfort: yogurt, rice pudding, a milk shake.

Use a fragrant candle or potpourri to freshen the air in your house, which takes in little fresh air in the winter.

If you don't already have one, buy a reading lamp for your bedside. Be sure you can turn it on and off without getting up.

Put warm lotion on your hands made rough and dry by the cold weather. Put the lotion in a pan or basin of very hot water for about 10 minutes and then soak up the soothing comfort of the warm lotion.

Go walking on a nature trail that you have only ever seen in the spring or summer. Appreciate the beauty that you wouldn't see in other seasons of the year.

Going out on a cold day? Start your car several minutes before you leave so it will be warm when you're ready to go.

Whenever it snows, go out in it while it is fresh—even while it is still snowing. A blanket of quiet will be falling on the earth. Let yourself be soothed by it.

Don't let the cold winter weather keep you inside altogether. Spend time outside, even if it's a short walk nearby. Dress warmly and venture out.

Put a flannel shirt on as soon as it comes out of the clothes dryer.

Cooking for one and eating alone can be difficult. Don't hesitate to rely on frozen dinners or prepared foods from a nearby grocery store or take-out restaurant.

Eat or drink something hot for breakfast —oatmeal, grits, cream of wheat, or cocoa.

If your usual eating habits are so disrupted that you're missing meals, set your alarm to go off around lunch or dinner time. What to eat? Drink a glass of juice while heating up a can of soup. Put the soup in a mug and add crumbled crackers. Eat it standing in the kitchen, just gazing out the window. It's okay. You've eaten.

Keep small boxes of cereal and pints of milk on hand. Eat it for lunch or dinner as well as breakfast.

Set a breakfast or lunch date with a friend who you are used to seeing by yourself—as opposed to someone you spent time with when you were part of a couple or as a family. It will be reassuring to be in a familiar situation with a friend, and it may avoid the discomfort of mixing your old and new lives.

Add orange slices to your menu to help replenish your supply of Vitamin C, which runs low in months when days are short.

Pack your lunch or supper first thing in the morning and put it in the refrigerator. It will be waiting for you whenever you're ready.

Make this quick vegetable soup for dinner: Sauté for 5 minutes in 2 tablespoons of olive oil, 1/4 cup diced carrots, 1/2 cup diced onions, 1/2 cup diced celery. Add 3 cups hot water or stock, 1 cup canned tomatoes, 1/2 cup peeled, diced potatoes, 1/4 cup barley, 1 tablespoon chopped parsley, 1/2 teaspoon salt, pepper to taste. Cover and simmer for about 35 minutes.

Select prepared foods, such as a rotisserie-style chicken, that will last for several meals. Eat the drumsticks at one meal and slice up the rest for sandwiches. Feeling energetic? Cook up the carcass in a soup.

After lunch, go for a 15-minute walk. It will revive you, and you'll be able to put in a productive afternoon.

Buy a box of Jello, several cans of soup, and some Tylenol on your next trip to the store to have on hand if you catch a winter cold or the flu.

Set your breakfast up before you go to bed: put water in the coffee pot or kettle and set the table. Put a book or magazine by your place setting. You'll be surprised at how cared for you feel when you get up in the morning.

Cook your favorite comfort food for dinner. Mashed potatoes, scrambled eggs, meat loaf, macaroni and cheese, or tuna casserole. Cook enough to have some leftovers.

Splurge on a pint of raspberries.

Check to see that you have the phone numbers of neighbors or relatives that you might need to reach in an emergency. Make sure that you have them both at your house, purse or wallet, and in your car. Give a spare house key to a neighbor.

Hide a $10 bill in a side pocket or your purse or wallet to have on hand in an emergency. The glove compartment of your car is another good hiding spot.

Lock the doors to your house when you're at home by yourself. You'll feel safe and secure.

Scheduling an annual cancer screening? Make the appointment for the first thing in the morning so you can get it over with early without giving anxiety a chance to build.

If your new journey began with the death of a spouse, resuming your normal routines won't seem normal at all. Take time to think of ways to manage these transitions, such as the suggestions that follow.

If friends and colleagues have taken up a collection for a memorial, consider a gift for the office, yours or your love's: a small tree for the courtyard or something that would make life more pleasant on a daily basis for people in the office.

If you must go back to work early on in your new journey, visit the office before your official return. Make sure you spend enough time to let all of your colleagues comfort you, and try to comfort them, too. You may need more than one visit. Talk about what you've been through. It's what you're really thinking about. Be honest. Tell them it's difficult but that you're trying.

Before you return to work in the office, do a small project from home. Work on it when you can.

Coordinate your return to work with your workload. Try working a Saturday before you return so you don't face a mountain of e-mail messages and a full mailbox on your first day back. Once back, ask for help. You'll get it.

Keep the memory of your love close at hand at the office. Put a framed photo or a prize trophy or plaque on your desk, use a well-used desk set or pen, and adopt their favorite coffee mug as your own.

Seasonal holidays—or any holiday meaningful to a family—can be difficult for you. Instead of observing the way you always have, meet with your family and friends and talk about how to make the best of a year when your hearts feel broken. Which past traditions are just too painful to endure this year? Which traditions do you want to hold on to even though you know they'll be difficult to face?

In planning your first holidays without your love, the key is to lower your expectations. Get plenty of rest, stay away from crowded shopping malls, decline invitations to parties that would be difficult to face, and cut down on your cooking and baking. This year, simplify. There will be many years in the future to resume what, for you, are your traditional holiday activities.

Check out an audio tape from your library on how to relax and relieve stress, and learn some techniques that might help you during a sleepless night.

Spend time in bed reading the newspaper.

Keep a radio with a tape player in your kitchen and listen to music or the news while you cook.

Rent a Bogart or Bogart/Bacall or Bogart/Hepburn film. Relax and enjoy watching it.

Read your own horoscope and check out those of close friends and relatives. Cut out one that fits someone you love and send it with a short note.

Take a vacation day tomorrow. Don't schedule anything, don't start a project, don't shop for groceries, don't clean your house, don't pay your bills. Take the day off to relax and revive.

Irish or not, celebrate St. Patrick's Day on March 17 by cooking a pot of corned beef, cabbage, and onions. Invite a friend to share or send a serving to a neighbor who's also alone.

Holidays that celebrate love—
Valentine's Day, Mother's Day, and
Father's Day—are difficult for people
making life-changing transitions. You
may want to stay away from the greet-
ing card racks altogether, but don't let
these days of love pass completely
unnoticed. Buy yourself some Valentine
candy, send a Mother's Day card to
someone who became a new mother
this year or a Father's Day card to a
favorite uncle or friend.

Visit a bookstore or your library and
choose an audio tape of a novel by your
favorite author. Listen to it during lunch
or at other times when you are alone.

Give a friend a labor of love: paint, sew, mend, make a needed repair, or otherwise give of your talents. Everyone has a gift; share yours.

Visit a flower shop and buy a stem or two of fresh flowers and put them where you'll see them often.

Visit an art gallery. If you can, find one with an exhibit of paintings depicting spring to remind yourself that better days are ahead.

Spring

MOVING TOWARD NEW LIFE

Where will your new journey lead?
Consider the possibility that
it can lead to a life where richness
and even love can grow again.
This spring section of comfort is meant to
prompt you gently on your path to your
new and different life. Many of these
comforts are close to home, for this is still
a time of inward focus. But the comforts
are also close to nature, which in the
Spring is so full of new life.
This is the season where new travelers
take their first steps toward new life.

Friends you spent time with when you were part of a couple or family will remain friends, but don't be surprised if their relationships change. You probably won't enjoy going to the same places as before because you'll feel like the third wheel, and your loss will feel fresh. Don't step away from your friends altogether, but do change your activities. Instead of the dinner foursome, try three for brunch or two for lunch.

Wear a piece of jewelry that belonged to or was a gift from someone you love. If a watch or ring isn't working or wearable, find a place to repair or reset it into a style that you can wear regularly.

Call or write to a friend who has moved away or a friend long out of touch.

At the annual dinner dance or office party, don't go alone but invite your son or your brother as your guest. Or team up with someone else who will be going alone. Create a new circle of companions, male and female, young and old.

Give a surprise long-distance call to an older friend or relative early in the morning when minds and outlooks are fresh.

Take a picture of your next visitor. How many pictures do you have of your closest friends?

How you feel on the inside and how you look on the outside may be two very different things. When people comment on how well you look and how well you seem to be coping, don't hesitate to tell them how difficult a time it is for you.

Send a card to a good friend who lives far away.

Appreciate the polite manner of men in their sixties and seventies. They're the ones who grew up holding doors, doffing hats, offering arms, and walking on the street-side of the sidewalk. You'll feel cared for, and they'll feel appreciated.

If you're going out with friends, arrange to car pool. That way you won't always have to come and go from your house alone.

Seek comfort from compassionate groups at your church, local hospital, or community center. Find support from people who are newly single or who have taken care of a dying family member. They are fellow travelers and together you will find comfort.

Set aside magazines and books that you just can't get through now but know you'll one day want to read.

Sit down with your weekly television schedule and find programs that you'd enjoy watching. Tape them for a Saturday night home alone or when there's nothing else on you might like to watch.

Read a book that you enjoyed ten or even twenty years ago. It will be reassuring to return to a familiar source of pleasure and comfort.

On the birthday of a beloved friend or relative no longer living, raise your spirits by calling someone who will easily remember the day and together you can share happy memories of birthdays past.

On one of the first warm days of spring, thoroughly air out your house. Open the windows and doors, and let the stale air out and the fresh air in.

In the spring of the year thoughts turn to summer vacations, and the prospect of a vacation without your usual traveling companion may be more than you can face. But don't let your new circumstances spoil vacation memories. Display photos and mementos from a favorite vacation from the past and enjoy having the memories close by. Watch your family's home videos from past vacations, too.

When you venture out on a vacation, let your first outing be in familiar and comfortable surroundings. Stay at a bed and breakfast in your old hometown. You'll know your way around, see some familiar faces, and find out what's new, too.

See how many varieties of birds you can find in and around your yard, and install a bird feeder if you don't already have one.

Buy an Adirondack Chair or a hammock —or any other kind of chair that is comfortable—for sitting outside and relaxing.

Locate a place to go pick your own strawberries. Pick a generous amount for eating now and enough to make a few jars
of strawberry jam that you will enjoy next
fall and winter when inexpensive, fresh
strawberries are a distant memory.

On a bright, cold day put your bedding
outside for a few hours on a clothesline
or a railing.

Fill a vase with whatever flowers are
blooming outside or with fresh cut
greens from your shrubs.

Sit outside with your back to the sun
and let the warmth relax your muscles.

Drive to a nearby state park and take a
walk along a stream. Notice all the vege-
tation that is emerging from the winter.

Savor the best part of spring—flowering
trees and shrubs. Don't let a day go by
without spending some time appreciat-
ing the varieties that live around you.

Put a night light in your hallway outlet to light your evening path. Your guests will appreciate it, too.

Splurge on a pair of 100 percent cotton pillowcases—whether you need new pillowcases or not. You'll find comfort every night when you lay your head down on a cool, soft pillow.

Start some seedlings inside for planting later on in your garden outside.

Get back into an exercise routine if you've let the cold weather keep you inside or if you haven't felt well enough to exercise. Spring is a great aid to energy and outlook.

Cook a big pot of one of your favorite soups and give a quart of it to a neighbor or a friend.

Try some fruit you haven't eaten before —like kiwi (peel and slice; the light green fruit is fragrant and not too sweet), mango (cut in half like a cantaloupe and scrape out the seeds; very sweet), or star fruit (cut crosswise, as if you were dicing a carrot, to get beautiful star-shaped bites of the sweet fruit).

Keep a pitcher of water in the refrigerator, and put a few slices of lemon in it. Reach for it instead of a soft drink.

Visit the best bakery you know and treat yourself to your favorite pastry.

Do you have a favorite restaurant that you frequented as a couple or a family on a regular basis? Go there, and tell the owners or your favorite waiter about your loss and that you'll be back soon. When you're ready to go back for a meal, order carry-out. When you do go back for full service, return for lunch or dessert with a friend rather than for dinner.

When you're ready to go back for dinner, call ahead and ask for a table for one, and take a book along to read while you're waiting.

Visit a new-to-you restaurant, one without memories attached.

Take a young friend out to eat. There's nothing like being around kids to make new life feel possible and welcome.

Take a few extra minutes to make your evening meal attractive as well as nutritious. Add color to your plate with a salad, and cut up an apple or an orange or add some grapes. Arrange the food attractively, and take time to enjoy it.

Going out to the grocery store? Ask a neighbor if you can pick up a needed item. Next time, they might do the same for you.

Invite a friend to share a meal. Purchase or prepare a simple cold pasta dish or salad, nothing elaborate, and spend just an hour or so together. You'll be satisfying two of your most basic needs—food and friendship.

Look into the laws in your state on living wills—how you wish to be treated medically in the event that you are unconscious or otherwise unable to make your wishes known. If you don't have a living will, execute one soon.

Check your supply of candles and flashlights in case you lose power during a thunderstorm.

On Memorial Day, visit the grave of a friend or relative and leave a small bouquet of flowers from your yard.

June 14 is Flag Day. Fly an American flag, even a small one. Sometime during the day, say the Pledge of Allegiance out loud.

Buy a book of stamps, writing paper, and envelopes, and when the house is quiet and there's no one to talk to, write a note to a friend or relative.

Never go to bed alone! Take along the companionship of a good book, interesting magazine, or letter from a friend.

Read the comics in the newspaper. If one strip reminds you of a friend, cut it out and send it. Humor is a welcome ingredient in all our lives.

For a midweek treat, do something out of the ordinary—go to a movie, rent a video, go out for ice cream, or pick up a special dessert.

Go with your church or community group to an art museum or a home and garden tour. You'll be uplifted by the art and the beautiful homes and gardens, and your companions could turn out to be new friends.

Pull over and watch a little league baseball practice.

After reading a particularly good contemporary book, write a thank you note to the author. Send it to the publisher listed in the front of the book, and it will be forwarded to an appreciative author.

Look for reruns of your favorite television programs and enjoy watching them; record them for viewing later.

If you walk regularly, break the routine of your usual route. You will see new sights and think new thoughts.

Rearrange a few favorite living room accessories—like a lamp or a painting or other work of art. You will look at them in a whole new way.

Mail a packet of seeds to a friend.

Tear out magazine and newspaper articles you're too busy to read. Tuck them away and read them next time you're waiting for the doctor, dentist, or drive-through bank teller.

Rescue a withering plant from a neighbor, nurse it back to health, and return it with a bow.

Take a photograph of the outside of your house. Send it to a grandchild or an out of town friend with an invitation to visit.

Swap magazines with a friend or neighbor.

Plant a tomato plant in a generous pot on a sunny porch and enjoy your own harvest.

Give new parents the newspaper from the day their baby was born. Put it in an airtight container and tie it with a pink or blue bow.

Think about taking a mini vacation to visit a friend or a relative. Make some inquiries and get something set up for the early summer.

Buy a guest book for your home or summer home. Ask all your visitors to sign the book and write a brief comment on their visit.

Break the monotony of your daily routine by driving home a different way and enjoy seeing something new.

Sit outside and read the newspaper.

Plan a special Sunday. Worship at a friend's church, and then treat him or her to breakfast afterwards. Next time, you'll be the one being treated to a Sunday out.

Rent a video of your favorite Rogers and Hammerstein musical, and watch it with a few friends who know and love it, too. Turn the lights down, the sound up, and sing along.

Take a day trip with a church or community group. Treat it like a new way to take a vacation and enjoy it.

Volunteer to be an overnight baby-sitter for a family you know. Your routine will be changed and you'll be doing something for someone else.

When you receive a compliment, savor it —then pass it on to someone else.

House-sit for a friend or neighbor while they take a short trip. Don't just take in the mail and water the plants, sit in their house for a while and read a good book or a magazine. Take your lunch and eat it there. You may end up feeling a little like you're the one who took the vacation.

Watch for a good dramatic or mystery series starting on television—probably on PBS. Tape episodes you can't watch, and watch them during a lull in your week or weekend.

Visit a bookstore or library and look at books about gardening and flowers. Start planning your spring garden.

Count your blessings.

Summer

A PAUSE IN THE JOURNEY

*Summer is a time to take a break
from day-to-day life, to have fewer
obligations, take a vacation,
and lead a slower-paced life.
On your new journey, summer is a
time to pause and take care of yourself.
In the Spring you glanced ahead to
new life, but the slower pace of summer
lets you take more time to rest,
reflect, and continue to heal.
The comforts in this section focus
on your physical comfort—staying cool
in warm temperatures as your
journey continues.*

What do you wish people would say to comfort you? Is it that you would like them to talk about your lost love? To share stories of happy times together? When people ask if there's anything they can do, tell them to share their memories.

Is there a low point in your day, a time when energy and spirits sag? Probably in the late afternoon? Make that a time to stop what you're doing for at least 10 or 15 minutes, sit or lie down, cover up with a soft blanket if it's cool, and listen to music that relaxes you. Drink a cup of herbal tea, ice tea, or whatever is tasty and soothing.

When a crying jag hits, find relief in your tears. It's a way of being cleansed of your pain.

Stay in touch by phone or mail with the people you find the most comforting: a favorite aunt or uncle whose company you have always enjoyed, a treasured friend or former roommate who could always help you, no matter what. You'll find comfort in knowing they are still there, with or without a crisis. Seek someone you know will make you smile.

Plan an outing that echoes the past. Make it an activity you might have done as a couple or with your parents when you were a child. Or do something that you know a favorite relative enjoyed. Did your dad have a favorite fishing spot? Did your mother enjoy a long drive to an out of town restaurant? Take comfort in the pleasantries of your past.

When you are sorting through old pictures, put away the ones that show the people you love in times of pain or distress or decline. Keep pictures from happier days accessible where you can look at them often.

Remember the anniversaries of painful events in the lives of your friends—the death of a child, a painful divorce, a bout with cancer, the wedding anniversary of a widow or a widower. Call them or send a note and tell them that you are thinking of them.

Just when you think your new journey is going well, something will trigger your pain when you're least expecting it. When painful memories come to call, take a look back through your journal to remind yourself how far you've come. Give yourself credit for making progress.

When you find yourself saying, "we used to…" remember that you still can. To remember is to love. Take that Sunday afternoon drive you always took. You'll be together in your thoughts and love.

Make a care package for a friend who is caring for someone in the hospital or at home. Put a small box of chocolates in it along with short articles, cartoons, photographs, or recipes that you know will interest them. You'll be providing a welcome respite from your friend's all too real trials.

Summers usually mean outdoor concerts. Look for an opportunity in your area to sit outside and listen to music.

Return to summers past to find relaxation for the present. How did you spend your time as a child in the summer—swimming, riding bicycles or horses, watching baseball or softball games? Whatever it was, do it again as an adult and return to a time in your life that was less stressful and more carefree.

On any trips you take, buy a small memento of an especially memorable place or experience. It can be a postcard, a piece of jewelry by a local artist, or a Christmas tree ornament that, come December, will bring back pleasant memories of the summer.

Will you be taking a long trip by car? Make sure you have something interesting or entertaining to listen to. If your car has a tape player, check out a variety of audiotapes from your library.

Pick some flowers from your yard and make a small arrangement for a neighbor or friend.

Take a cool bath or shower before bed to cool off at the end of a hot day.

While on a vacation to your old hometown, visit the parents of your good friends—even if your friends themselves have moved away.

Keep an up-to-date atlas and an almanac in the house to help summer guests decide on the best routes to take and to find answers to questions as they come up.

Go to a lake, the ocean, or a creek and sit and watch the water. Experience all the senses you can—sound, smell, sight, and let the rhythm of the water's movement relax you.

Take a walk regularly in the coolest part of the day—whether it's morning or evening.

Rise just a little earlier than usual and work in your garden when it's cool and quiet.

Make this simple spicy Gazpacho soup:
8 to 12 ounces of tomato or
    vegetable-style tomato juice
8 ounce jar of mild salsa
One can light or white beans
Approximately one-quarter cup each of
    cucumber, onion, and bell pepper.
Mix the tomato juice and the salsa.
Drain the beans, chop the vegetables.
Add to juice mixture, cover, and chill.
Serve with a wedge of lime for garnish
or squeeze generously for more flavor.
Tastes even better the next day.

Go to a movie matinee to escape the
afternoon heat.

Sit outside on a dark porch or yard,
and, for an inning or two, tune in a
baseball game on the radio. You don't
even have to know anything about
baseball or care what's going on in the
game. A good announcer will entertain
you with talk of politics, human nature,
geography, and food. And all the while

you'll be in your own peaceful world under the stars. Besides, someone you know—a friend or relative—is a baseball fan, and knowing what's going on will help you stay connected with them.

Use water in whatever way it is soothing to you. Go for a swim, soak your feet in warm water, or soak in the bathtub.

Put a roll of film in your camera. Take a photograph of your own garden or of a favorite garden when they're at their peak. Keep the photos to look at sometime next winter.

In the heat of the summer, close the blinds on the windows that get the afternoon sun.

Did you return from a summer vacation with a new print or photograph? Take it in to be framed or measure it and buy a ready-made frame for it.

After a good summer rain has cooled the air, open doors and windows and bring some cooler air inside.

As summer draws to a close, make sure you haven't neglected any of your usual summer rituals. Do you make an annual visit to a certain amusement park? Take a picnic to a favorite spot? Eat ice cream from a well-loved establishment? Don't let old customs fall by the wayside.

Poke a peppermint stick into a lemon and serve it to a young friend. Have one for yourself, too.

Keep plenty of salad materials on hand—lettuce, bell peppers, cucumbers, tomatoes, and carrots—so you can make a cold salad instead of a hot meal when it feels much too hot to cook.

Buy fresh peaches, tomatoes, corn, or raspberries and enjoy them as often as possible. They aren't available all year; enjoy them while you can.

Take yourself out to your favorite restaurant and order your favorite dish.

Eat breakfast outside to be closer to morning's beauty.

Visit a candy store that sells candy you ate as a child. Pick out a bag of your favorite kinds, and send a friend or relative his or her favorites, too.

Eat a bowl of fresh raspberries for breakfast.

Late on a hot summer afternoon, pour yourself a cold beverage and sit and enjoy it in the coolest part of your house.

Keep a dish of Starlight mints handy for a quick pick-me-up.

Drink your favorite beverages out of your favorite cups and glasses. Have your tea in the cup your grandmother gave you, or pour a glass of wine in your good crystal.

On Independence Day, listen to a march by John Philip Sousa.

Read your favorite poem. Memorize it, one line a day. Recite it aloud.

Six months have passed since the holiday season. Summon up the spirit of the holidays by visiting an elderly or ill person in a hospital or nursing home.

Read a Dear Abby or Ann Landers advice column in the newspaper. It never hurts to get some advice and hear other people's troubles. They may make yours seem small by comparison.

Start a list of the very best books you've ever read, and add to it as you discover new ones. That way you'll have good books to recommend to friends and to go back and enjoy again.

Buy a small gift ($1-$2) for a child you know—a niece, nephew, grandchild, or neighbor. Or invite a child out for a treat—for ice cream or to a fast food restaurant. It's an investment in self-esteem for the child and in a friendship for you.

Rent a video that will make you laugh. The Marx Brothers' "Horsefeathers" is a good candidate, or choose your favorite comedian. Sit back, relax, and—even if you are alone—laugh!

Are you grateful for the guidance and influence of a certain teacher or mentor? Tell them how much they have meant to you, and thank them. It will be your gift in return.

If your library has an audio section, borrow tapes or compact discs from it frequently. Listen to familiar music or explore new music. Unfamiliar with classical? Try a symphony by Haydn (there are 120 of them) or Beethoven (he wrote nine) or Mozart (whose music has actually been shown to make people perform better on tests!). Or make a selection based on an instrument you enjoy hearing—piano, violin, classical guitar, organ, etc.

Leave a message on a busy friend's answering machine even if you know no one is home. The message? I hope you are well, I miss seeing you, and just wanted to say hello.

Take a cutting from favorite plant. Root it, plant it, and give it to someone special.

Move a picture that hangs in your living room into your bedroom and vice versa. If you switch pictures around you'll look at them in new ways.

Get a subscription by mail to your hometown newspaper.

Get started on a good book. Go to the library and check out a half a dozen that look promising. If you don't like one, move to the next. Never be without something good to read. Try an art book or a travel guide. You don't have to read every word; just browse through it.

If you have a health concern—even if you think it's a minor one, make an appointment with a doctor and discuss it with him or her. If you think the doctor is not sympathetic or responsive, go to another doctor. Find someone who will give you the care you need.

When you buy stamps at the post office, ask to see the special commemorative issues that are available. They add a nice touch to the outside of a letter or card, especially when you are sending a special message to someone.

In one column, make a list of four or five activities you enjoy. In a second column, write down how often you've done the activity in the last five years. Have you neglected things you really enjoy?

Take a musical trip to the best times in your life by listening to your then-favorite music—whether that means Irving Berlin, Elvis, the Beatles, or Sinatra.

Be helpful to a neighbor. Drive a car-pool leg, bake them dessert, invite their toddler to your house for a short visit, share flowers from your garden, books, and magazines.

Say no! Take care of yourself by spending time on activities and people that you enjoy and saying no to those you don't—for whatever reason.

Touch someone's cheek with the backs of your fingers. Find the youngest and softest cheek around. Or the oldest.

Fall

LIVING INTO YOUR NEW LIFE

*There were hints of new life in the
spring of your new journey, and in the
fall more change evolves. The shape and
substance of your new life will be
coming into focus, and you may be
ready to move on to new experiences
and build relationships with
people new in your life.*

*Don't misunderstand. This may not
come in the first year of your journey;
it may be several years in coming.
Comforts for the fall of your journey
will help you look ahead, encourage
you to find new experiences, reach out,
and move forward.*

Do the falling leaves make your spirits sag? You aren't alone. Fall is a difficult time of year for many people because the dying of leaves remind us so poignantly of our own losses. Try to keep your feelings in perspective and remember that it will eventually give way to other seasons of new life.

Make a list of all you are thankful for.

Sit down and write a thank you note to someone who has been particularly sensitive to you during your new journey. Tell them how much you have appreciated their friendship and love.

On your birthday, light a candle. Save it, and on the birthday of someone special in your life, light it again.

Call a friend who is coping with a difficult situation to lend support and sympathy.

On the anniversary of the day your new journey began, the day your life changed completely, plan a special day to celebrate your loved one's life. Choose a favorite hobby or volunteer activity and build around it. Was your love an avid gardener? Then plant a special tree in your yard or make a donation to a public garden. Did your love have a favorite charitable cause? Make a special donation in his or her name. Don't let the day pass without remembering this special life.

Feeling blue? Listen to music that expresses sadness more profoundly than words ever could. Try one of these by Beethoven: second movement of the Piano Concerto No. 5; second movement of Symphony No. 6, the Pastoral Symphony.

Of all the seasons, fall has some of the most dramatic sights. Pause to look at some beautiful fall colors and be thankful for their beauty.

Now that fall is here, put a soft blanket at the foot of your bed or on the back of the sofa for times when you feel cool.

Invest in spring. Pick out some daffodil or tulip bulbs and plant them now.

Launder your old, comfortable bathrobe and wrap yourself up in it on cool fall evenings and mornings. Is it frayed and showing signs of wear? So much the better. Be comforted by something so familiar.

Are fall nights getting cool where you live? Put a set of flannel sheets on your bed. If you don't have any, put them on your Christmas list!

Collect a handful of the most beautiful gold and red leaves that you can find when you're out on a fall walk, and buy a few small gourds on your next trip to the grocery store. Arrange them in a basket or bowl on your dining room table. Savor the beauty of fall every time you walk through the room.

Carve a pumpkin. Put it on your porch.

Don't let the full moon go unnoticed. When it gets to its fullest, enjoy a walk in the evening by the moonlight or just a glance from your porch or balcony.

Catch a fresh breeze for your bedroom. Leave a window open just a crack to keep the room fresh and bring you the fresh scent of the out-of-doors.

Take a drive to a place where you can look out over a hillside or a mountain of changing autumn colors. Stop, look, listen, relax, and feel a sense of calm from one of nature's most beautiful sights.

Buy a hooded sweatshirt and wear it with the hood up when working outside on a cold day.

Keep a spare umbrella or pair of gloves in your car—whichever will best take care of you in your particular climate.

Dress warmly. Add an extra layer on cool days—a turtleneck or T-shirt, tights, or insulated underwear.

Shop at a store with a good selection of fresh produce, and enjoy its color and aroma. Treat yourself to the waning crops of summer—tomatoes, peaches, corn—or whatever you know will soon be unavailable.

Eat in your dining room tonight. Be sure to light the candles and use a cloth napkin.

Make homemade applesauce for breakfast. Peel and cube two apples, place in a saucepan, and partly cover with water. Simmer until tender. Depending on sweetness of apples, add enough sugar to make them palatable and cook for about 3 more minutes. Sprinkle with cinnamon, lemon juice. Cool slightly and enjoy with toast.

Buy a packet or two of yeast so you can bake bread, dinner rolls, or cinnamon rolls. Enjoy them fresh, freeze some, and share with friends and neighbors.

Visit an orchard and pick your own apples or buy a bag of fresh local apples from a produce stand.

Think of a favorite dish or dessert that your mother or grandmother or favorite aunt used to make on special occasions—a cherry pie, bread pudding, banana bread. Enjoy making it for yourself and share it with friends.

Clip a buy-one-get-one-free coupon for ice cream or a meal and invite a friend for an inexpensive outing.

Donate canned or dry food items to a project that feeds the hungry.

On a cold morning, put a slice of lemon in a cup of hot water. Few drinks are as soothing and warming.

Cook a meatless pasta dish for dinner. Use your favorite recipe or try this one for pasta and tomatoes:

> 2 T. olive oil
> 1 clove garlic, sliced paper thin
> 1 t. chopped jalapeno pepper
> 2 plum tomatoes, diced
> 1/2 cup chicken broth
> 2 T. flat-leaf parsley, chopped
> 1/2 pound cooked pasta—spaghetti or fettuccine
> green olives

Heat olive oil, add garlic, and cook for 1 minute. Add peppers, tomatoes, broth, and parsley and cook over moderate heat for 3-4 minutes. Meanwhile, cook pasta, drain, and toss with tomato mixture. Garnish with basil leaves and green olives.

Buy boxes of assorted herbal and regular teas to have on hand for a friend who stops by on a cold day.

Cook baked potatoes for dinner. Using the oven for an hour and a half will help heat your house on a cold day.

Eat a few squares of a chocolate bar for dessert.

Tired of cooking the same old meals? Make it a point to visit your library (or a newsstand) and look through some magazines to spot some new dishes that sound tempting. Jot down a few recipes and try them soon. Buy a new cookbook with recipes for single people. *Serves One* by Toni Lydecker is a good one.

Look ahead to Thanksgiving. How will it be different this year? What part of it will be most difficult for you? Are there changes that you can make that would make the day easier to cope with? Discuss your feelings with the people who are traditionally together at your Thanksgiving dinner.

On Thanksgiving, give thanks for the people you love and those you will come to love.

Look through old family pictures, and you're bound to find a photograph of a family member in uniform. On Veteran's Day remember your favorite Vet.

Arrange to go out to a class or a group that meets at least once a month, whether it is to play bridge, bowl, sing, tap dance, learn something new, volunteer, or just have lunch.

Invite a friend to come watch a video or a movie you'll both enjoy. If you don't have a VCR but you have a friend who does, suggest that you watch a movie together and volunteer to be the one to rent the movie and bring the snack.

Call the Red Cross and arrange to give blood. Giving life to someone else may lift your own spirits.

Make a list of your favorite people's birthdays and post it in a place where you'll see it every day. As the months go by, be sure to send cards or make calls.

Stay in touch with other families in your neighborhood by supporting the children's school activities—bake sales, fairs, and games.

Recommend a good book to a friend—and ask for a recommendation in return.

Buy a $5 phone card and send it to a friend, niece, nephew, or a favorite college student—someone you'd like to hear from.

Read an autobiography of someone you admire.

Think ahead about the possibility of next year's travels. Who haven't you seen that you would like to visit? Might you take a trip in the summer? Think about where you've been, where you'd like to revisit, and where you'd like to go for the first time.